The Colourscape Chunky Collection

14 Designs by Sarah Hatton
Introducing Colourscape Chunky by Kaffe Fassett

The thing that inspired me the most when faced with designing colourscape yarn was the long colour repeat. The yarn embraces the revival of wonderful old techniques in spinning that involve real craftmanship. To see colours fed in to machinery in handfuls of pure colour creating the subtle colourscape blends was very stimulating.

I wanted the palette to be very wearable, from deep mysterious tones of purples, maroons and turquoise to the softness of dusty pastels. Given my idiosyncratic colouring instructions the technicians did a brilliant job of blending our final moods.

Kaffe Fassett

Valour in Ghost

Entice
in Heath

Flutter
in Cherry

Jinx
in Frosty

Tender
in Candy Pink

Sigh
in Frosty

Glow
in Cherry

Tainted
in Frosty

Solace
in Ghost

Smoulder
in Northern Lights

Ombre
in Cherry

Grace
in Northern Lights

Tempo
in Carnival

The Yarn

Kaffe chooses his palette by taking different shades of yarn and knotting them together to inspire the final blend of colours.

With Kaffe supervising, the dyed to match wool roving was hand thrown into a trough in his chosen sequences. All wool roving is weighted and measured by hand for accuracy and the process involves careful watching and guiding to make this yarn as Kaffe envisgaed.

This very unique process is slow, only 300 kilos per machine can be produced in a week. This hands on process uses very special machinery, tooled exclusively for Rowan in Yorkshire, England. After the wool is blended, the yarn is spun, as specified by Kaffe into a soft shetland-like twist for a good handle and generous length. The colours are vibrant in daylight and bring excitement to every stitch.

ROWAN
Colourscape
chunky
BY KAFFE FASSETT
100% LAMBSWOOL

The Colours

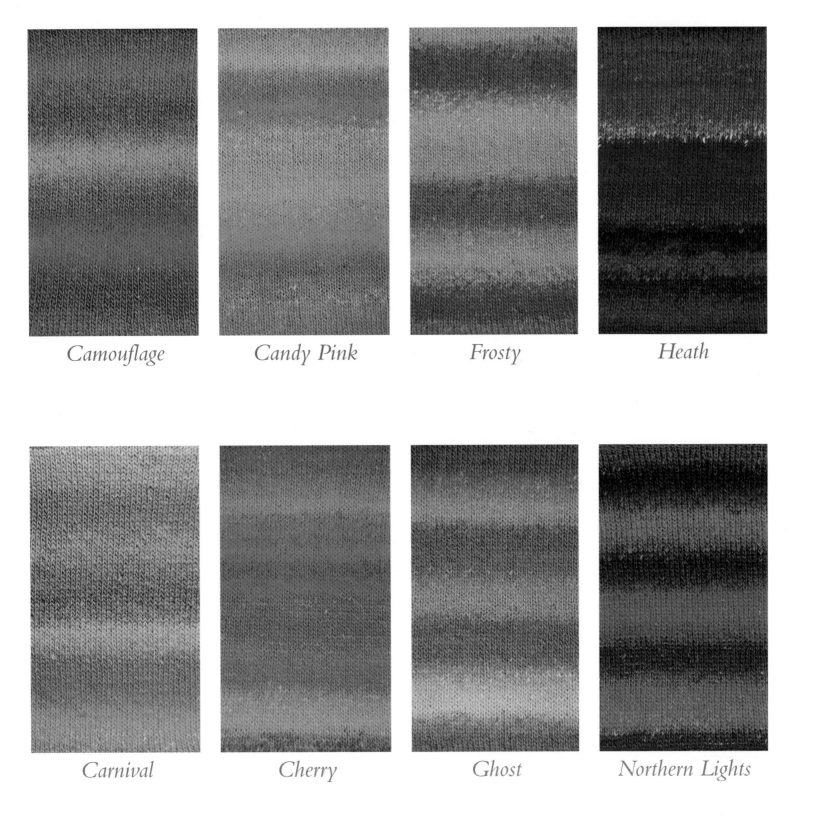

Camouflage

Candy Pink

Frosty

Heath

Carnival

Cherry

Ghost

Northern Lights

Gallery

Valour   48   Entice   28   Glow   32

Dandy   26   Sigh   38   Tainted   50

Tender   46   Grace   34

Smoulder   40   Solace   42   Flutter   30

Jinx   36   Ombre   35   Tempo   44

Dandy

SIZE

	S	M	L	XL	XXL	
To fit bust						
	81–86	91–96	102–107	112–117	122–127	cm
	32–34	36–38	40–42	44–46	48–50	in

YARN

Rowan Colourscape

5	6	6	7	8	x 100gm

(photographed in 437 Camouflage)

NEEDLES

1 pair 7mm (no 2) (USA 10½) needles
1 pair 6mm (USA 10) needles
Stitch holder

TENSION

14 sts and 18 rows to 10cm measured over st st using 7mm (no 2)
(USA 10½) needles.

BACK

Using 6mm (USA 10) needles cast on 65 [73: 81: 89: 99] sts.
Row 1 (RS): ★ K1, P1, rep from ★ to last st, K1.
Row 2: P1, ★ K1, P1, rep from ★ to end.
Row 3: As row 2.
Row 4: As row 1.
These 4 rows form patt.
Work 12 rows more in patt, ending with RS facing for next row.
Change to 7mm (USA 10½) needles.
Beg with a K row, cont in st st until back meas 32 [33: 34: 35: 36] cm, ending with RS facing for next row.
Shape armholes
Cast off 2 [4: 4: 5: 5] sts at beg of next 2 rows.
61 [65: 73: 79: 89] sts.
Dec 1 st at each end of next 3 [5: 7: 7: 9] rows, then 2 [1: 1: 2: 2] foll alt rows. 51 [53: 57: 61: 67] sts.
Cont straight until armholes meas 20 [21: 22: 23: 24] cm, ending with RS facing for next row.
Shape shoulders
Next row (RS): Cast off 5 [6: 6: 7: 8] sts, K until there are 9 [9: 10: 11: 12] sts on right needle, turn and leave rem sts on a stitch holder.
Work each side of neck separately.
Next row: Cast off 3 sts, P to end.
Cast off rem 6 [6: 7: 8: 9] sts.

With RS facing rejoin yarn to rem sts, cast off centre 23 [23: 25: 25: 27] sts, K to end.
Complete to match first side reversing shaping

LEFT FRONT

Using 6mm (USA 10) needles cast on 44 [48: 52: 56: 61] sts.
Row 1 (RS): ★ K1, P1, rep from ★ to last 2 [2: 2: 2: 1] sts, K1, P1 [1: 1: 1: 0].
Row 2: P1 [1: 1: 1: 0], K1, ★ P1, K1, rep from ★ to end.
Row 3: As row 2.
Row 4: As row 1.
These 4 rows form patt.
Work 12 rows more in patt, ending with RS facing for next row.
Change to 7mm (USA 10½) needles.
Next row (RS): K to last 13 sts, turn and leave rem 13 sts on a stitch holder for left front edging.
Next row: Purl. 31 [35: 39: 43: 48] sts.
Beg with a K row, cont in st st until left front matches back to shape armholes, ending with RS facing for next row.
Shape armhole
Next row (RS): Cast off 2 [4: 4: 5: 5] sts, K to end.
29 [31: 35: 38: 43] sts.
Work 1 row.
Dec 1 st at armhole edge of next 3 [5: 7: 7: 9] rows, then on foll 2 [1: 1: 2: 2] alt rows. 24 [25 27: 29: 32] sts.

Cont straight until 7 [7: 9: 9: 11] rows less have been worked than on back to shape shoulders, ending with **WS** facing for next row.

Shape neck

Next row (WS): Cast off 9 sts, P to end.

15 [16: 18: 20: 23] sts.

Dec 1 st at neck edge on next 3 rows, then 1 [1: 2: 2: 3] foll alt rows. 11 [12: 13: 15: 17] sts.

Work 1 row, ending with RS facing for next row.

Shape shoulder

Next row (RS): Cast off 5 [6: 6: 7: 8] sts, patt to end.

Work 1 row.

Cast off rem 6 [6: 7: 8: 9] sts.

RIGHT FRONT

Using 6mm (USA 10) needles cast on 44 [48: 52: 56: 61] sts.

Row 1 (RS): P1 [1: 1: 1: 0], ★ K1, P1, rep from ★ to last st, K1.

Row 2: K1, ★ P1, K1, rep from ★ to last 1 [1: 1: 1: 0] st, P1 [1: 1: 1: 0].

Row 3: As row 2.

Row 4: As row 1.

These 4 rows form patt.

Work 12 rows more in patt, ending with RS facing for next row.

Change to 7mm (USA 10½) needles.

Next row (RS): Patt 13 and leave these sts on a stitch holder for right front edging, K to end.

Next row: Purl. 31 [35: 39: 43: 48] sts.

Complete to match left front reversing shapings.

SLEEVES (BOTH ALIKE)

Using 6mm (USA 10) needles cast on 31 [33: 33: 33: 35] sts.

Work 12 rows in patt as given for back, ending with RS facing for next row.

Change to 7mm (USA 10½) needles.

Beg with a K row cont in st st shaping sides by inc 1 st at each end of 3rd row, then every foll 6th row to 49 [49: 47: 47: 49] sts, then every foll 8th row to 51 [53: 53: 53: 55] sts.

Cont straight until sleeve meas 44 [45: 46: 46: 46] cm, ending with RS facing for next row.

Shape top

Cast off 2 [4: 4: 5: 5] sts at beg of next 2 rows.

47 [45: 45: 43: 45] sts.

Dec 1 st at each end of next 5 [3: 3: 1: 1] rows then 1 [4: 6: 8: 8] foll alt rows, then every row to 25 [25: 25: 23: 23] sts.

Cast off 8 [8: 8: 7: 7] sts at beg of next 2 rows.

Cast off rem 9 sts.

MAKING UP

Press as described on the information page.

Join side and shoulder seams using back stitch or mattress stitch if preferred.

Left front edging

With RS facing using 6mm (USA 10) needles, rejoin yarn to 13 sts left on a stitch holder and cont in patt until left front edging is long enough when slightly stretched to to fit up left front to neck shaping, ending with RS facing for next row.

Cast off. Slip stitch in position.

Right front edging

With **WS** facing using 6mm (USA 10) needles rejoin yarn to 13 sts left on a stitch holder and cont in patt until 4 rows less have been worked than on left front edging to cast off, ending with RS facing for next row.

Next row (RS): Patt 2 sts, cast off 2 sts (to make buttonhole), patt to end.

Next row: Patt to end casting on 2 sts over 2 sts cast off on last row.

Work 2 rows, ending with RS facing for next row.

Cast off. Slip stitch in position.

Neckband

With RS facing using 6mm (USA 10) needles, cast on 11 sts, pick up and knit 19 [19: 21: 21: 22] sts up right side of neck from beg of st st, 23 [25: 25: 27: 27] sts from back neck and 30 [30: 32: 32: 33] sts down left side of neck and across front edging. 83 [85: 89: 91: 93] sts.

Beg with row 2 of patt work 3 rows more in patt, ending with RS facing for next row.

Next row (RS): Patt 2 sts, cast off 2 sts (to make buttonhole), patt to end.

Next row: Patt to end casting on 2 sts over 2 sts cast off on last row.

Work 4 rows, ending with RS facing for next row.

Cast off

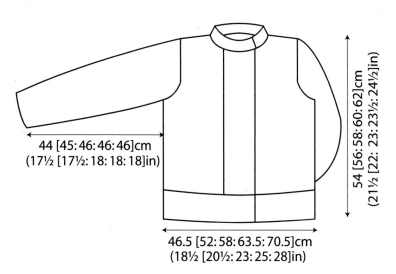

44 [45: 46: 46: 46]cm
(17½ [17½: 18: 18: 18]in)

54 [56: 58: 60: 62]cm
(21½ [22: 23: 23½: 24½]in)

46.5 [52: 58: 63.5: 70.5]cm
(18½ [20½: 23: 25: 28]in)

Entice

SIZE

	S	M	L	XL	XXL	
To fit bust						
	81–86	91–96	102–107	112–117	122–127	cm
	32–34	36–38	40–42	44–46	48–50	in

YARN

Rowan Colourscape

7	8	9	9	10	x 100gm

(photographed in 432 Heath)

NEEDLES

1 pair 7mm (no 2) (USA 10½) needles
Stitch holders

TENSION

14 sts and 18 rows to 10cm measured over st st using 7mm (no 2) (USA 10½) needles.

BODY (Worked sideways in 1 piece beg at right front opening edge)
Using 7mm (USA 10½) needles cast on 93 [95: 99: 103: 107] sts.
Row 1 (RS): ★ K1, P1, rep from ★ to last st, K1.
Row 2: P1, ★ K1, P1, rep from ★ to end.
These 2 rows form 1x1 rib.
Work 2 rows more in rib, ending with RS facing for next row.
Row 1 (RS): K1, (K1, P1) twice, K to last 5 sts, (P1, K1) twice, K1.
Row 2: K1, (P1, K1) twice, P to last 5 sts, (K1, P1) twice, K1.
These 2 rows form patt.
Cont in patt until work meas 51 [53: 55: 57: 59]cm, ending with RS facing for next row.
Shape right armhole
★★ **Next row (RS)**: Patt 25 sts and turn, leaving rem sts on a stitch holder.
Work a further 6 rows on these 25 sts only, ending with **WS** facing for next row.
Break yarn and leave these sts on a second holder.
Return to sts left on first holder, rejoin yarn with RS facing, cast off 29 [31: 33: 35: 37] sts, patt to end.
39 [39: 41: 43: 45] sts.
Dec 1 st at end of next row and at same edge on foll row.
37 [37: 39: 41: 43] sts.
Inc 1 st at beg of next row and at same edge on foll row.
39 [39: 41: 43: 45] sts.

Next row (WS): Patt 39 [39: 41: 43: 45] sts of lower section, turn and cast on 29 [31: 33: 35: 37] sts and patt across 25 sts left on second holder.
93 [95: 99: 103: 107] sts. ★★
Cont straight until work meas 34.5 [36.5: 39.5: 42.5: 45.5] cm from armhole cast on edge, ending with RS facing for next row.
Shape left armhole
Work as given for right armhole from ★★ to ★★.
Cont straight until work meas 49 [51: 53: 55: 57] cm from left armhole cast on edge, ending with RS facing for next row.
Work 4 rows in 1x1 rib. Cast off in rib.

SLEEVES
Using 7mm (USA 10½) needles cast on 33 [35: 37: 39: 41] sts.
Work 4 rows in 1x1 rib as given for back.
Beg with a K row cont in st st shaping sides by inc 1 st at each end of 3rd row, then every foll 4th row to 49 [49: 49: 51: 53] sts, then every foll 6th row to 61 [63: 65: 67: 69] sts.
Cont straight until sleeve meas 45 [46: 47: 47: 47] cm, ending with RS facing for next row.
Shape top
Dec 1 st at each end of next 2 rows. 57 [59: 61: 63: 65] sts.
Cast off 10 sts at beg of next 2 rows.
Cast off rem 37 [39: 41: 43: 45] sts.
MAKING UP

Press as described on the information page.
Join sleeve seams using back stitch or mattress stitch if preferred.
Matching top of sleeve seam to base of armhole and centre of sleeve cast off edge to centre of armhole top row-end edge, sew sleeves into armholes.

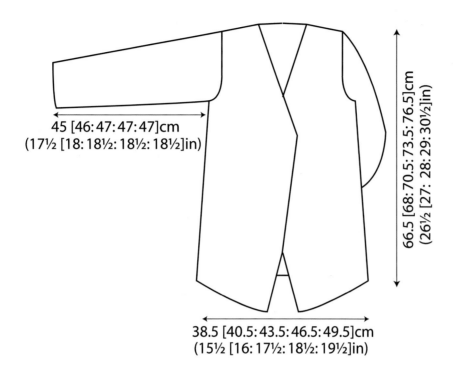

45 [46: 47: 47: 47]cm
(17½ [18: 18½: 18½: 18½]in)

66.5 [68: 70.5: 73.5: 76.5]cm
(26½ [27: 28: 29: 30½]in)

38.5 [40.5: 43.5: 46.5: 49.5]cm
(15½ [16: 17½: 18½: 19½]in)

Flutter

SIZE

	S	M	L	XL	XXL	
To fit bust						
	81–86	91–96	102–107	112–117	122–127	cm
	32–34	36–38	40–42	44–46	48–50	in

YARN

Rowan Colourscape

	S	M	L	XL	XXL	
	8	8	9	10	11	x 100gm

(photographed in Cherry 431)

NEEDLES

1 pair 7mm (no 2) (USA 10½) needles
1 pair 6mm (no 4) (USA 10) needles
6mm (no 4) (USA 10) circular needle
Stitch holder

TENSION

14 sts and 18 rows to 10cm measured over st st using 7mm (no 2) (USA 10½) needles.

BACK

Using 6mm (USA 10) needles cast on 72 [80: 88: 96: 106] sts.
Work 4 rows in garter st, ending with RS facing for next row.
Change to 7mm (USA 10½) needles.
Beg with a K row cont in st st until back meas 50 [51: 52: 53: 54] cm, ending with RS facing for next row.

Shape armholes

Cast off 4 [6: 6: 6: 6] sts at beg of next 2 rows.
64 [68: 76: 84: 94] sts.
Dec 1 st at each end of next 5 [5: 7: 9: 11] rows, then foll 2 alt rows. 50 [54: 58: 62: 68] sts.
Cont straight until armholes meas 21 [22: 23: 24: 25] cm, ending with RS facing for next row.

Shape shoulders

Next row (RS): Cast off 4 [5: 6: 7: 8] sts, K until there are 8 [9: 9: 10: 11] sts on right needle, turn and leave rem sts on a stitch holder.
Work each side of neck separately.
Next row: Cast off 3 sts, P to end.
Cast off rem 5 [6: 6: 7: 8] sts.
With RS facing rejoin yarn to rem sts, cast off centre 26 [26: 28: 28: 30] sts, P to end.
Complete to match first side reversing shaping

LEFT FRONT

Using 6mm (USA 10) needles cast on 24 [28: 32: 36: 41] sts.

Work 4 rows in garter st, ending with RS facing for next row.
Change to 7mm (USA 10½) needles.
Beg with a K row, cont in st st until left front matches back to shape armholes.

Shape armhole and neck

Next row (RS): Cast off 4 [6: 6: 6: 6] sts, K to last 2 sts, K2tog.
19 [21: 25: 29: 34] sts.
Work 1 row.
Dec 1 st at beg of next 5 [5: 7: 9: 11] rows, then on foll 2 alt rows **and at same time** dec 1 st at neck edge in 5th row, then 0 [0: 1: 1: 1] foll 6th row. 11 [13: 14: 16: 19] sts.
Dec 1 st at neck edge only on 2nd [2nd: 6th: 4th: 2nd] row, then 1 [1: 1: 1: 2] foll 6th rows. 9 [11: 12: 14: 16] sts.
Cont straight until left front matches back to shape shoulders, ending with RS facing for next row.

Shape shoulder

Next row (RS): Cast off 4 [5: 6: 7: 8] sts, patt to end.
Work 1 row.
Cast off rem 5 [6: 6: 7: 8] sts.

RIGHT FRONT

Work as given for left front reversing shapings.

SLEEVES (BOTH ALIKE)

Using 6mm (USA 10) needles cast on 31 [33: 33: 33: 35] sts.
Work 4 rows in garter stitch, ending with RS facing for next row.

Change to 7mm (USA 10½) needles.
Beg with a K row cont in st st shaping sides by inc 1 st at each end of 5th row, then every foll 6th row to 39 [39: 37: 37: 39] sts, then every foll 8th row to 51 [53: 53: 53: 55] sts.
Cont straight until sleeve meas 47 [48: 49: 49: 49] cm, ending with RS facing for next row.

Shape top
Cast off 4 [6: 6: 6: 6] sts at beg of next 2 rows.
43 [41: 41: 41: 43] sts.
Dec 1 st at each end of next 7 [5: 3: 1: 3] rows, then 8 [11: 13: 15: 15] foll alt rows, then every row to 7 sts.
Cast off rem 7 sts.

MAKING UP
Press as described on the information page.
Place marker at centre back neck.

Right collar
With RS facing, using 6mm (USA 10) or circular needle if required, pick up and knit 120 [124: 128: 132: 136] sts evenly up right front and around neck to centre back marker.
Row 1 (WS): ★K2, P2, rep from ★ to end.
This row sets rib.
Work 4cm in rib, ending with RS facing for next row.
Next row: Rib 82 [84: 88: 92: 94], K1, turn and leave rem sts on a stitch holder.
Cont on these 83 [85: 89: 93: 95] sts only.
Next row: K1, rib to end.
Last 2 rows set rib and garter stitch.
Cont as set until collar meas 20cm, ending with RS facing for next row. Cast off in rib.
With RS facing rejoin yarn to rem sts.
Next row: K1, rib to end.

Next row: Rib to last st, K1.
Last 2 rows set rib and garter stitch.
Cont as set until collar meas 20cm, ending with RS facing for next row. Cast off in rib.

Left collar
With RS facing, using 6mm (USA 10) or circular needle if required, pick up and knit 120 [124: 128: 132: 136] sts evenly down left front from centre back marker.
Row 1 (WS): ★ P2, K2, rep from ★ to end.
This row sets rib.
Work 4cm in rib, ending with RS facing for next row.
Next row: Rib 36 [36: 38: 38: 40], K1, turn and leave rem sts on a stitch holder.
Cont on these 37 [37: 39: 39: 41] sts only.
Next row: K1, rib to end.
Last 2 rows set rib and garter stitch.
Cont as set until collar meas 20cm, ending with RS facing for next row. Cast off in rib.
With RS facing rejoin yarn to rem sts.
Next row: K1, rib to end.
Next row: Rib to last st, K1.
Last 2 rows set rib and garter stitch.
Cont as set until collar meas 20cm, ending with RS facing for next row. Cast off in rib.
Join back neck seam.

Belt
Using 6mm (USA 10) needles cast on 10 sts.
Row 1 (RS): (K2, P2) 4 times, K2.
Row 2: P2, (K2, P2) 4 times.
These 2 rows form rib.
Cont in rib until belt meas 110 [120: 130: 140: 150] cm, ending with RS facing for next row. Cast off in rib.

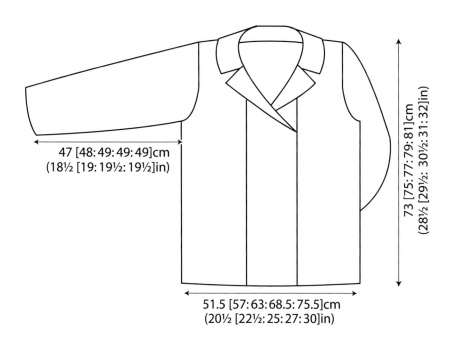

47 [48: 49: 49: 49]cm
(18½ [19: 19½: 19½]in)

73 [75: 77: 79: 81]cm
(28½ [29½: 30½: 31: 32]in)

51.5 [57: 63: 68.5: 75.5]cm
(20½ [22½: 25: 27: 30]in)

Glow

SIZE

	S	M	L	XL	XXL	
To fit bust						
	81–86	91–96	102–107	112–117	122–127	cm
	32–34	36–38	40–42	44–46	48–50	in

YARN
Rowan Colourscape

5	6	6	7	7	x 100gm

(photographed in 431 Cherry)

NEEDLES
1 pair 7mm (no 2) (USA 10½) needles
1 pair 6mm (no 4) (USA 10) needles
7mm (no 2) (USA 10½) circular needle
6mm (no 4) (USA 10) circular needle
Stitch holder

TENSION
14 sts and 18 rows to 10cm measured over st st using 7mm (no 2) (USA 10½) needles.

BACK
Using 6mm (USA 10) needles cast on 69 [77: 85: 93: 103] sts.
Row 1 (RS): ★ K1, P1, rep from ★ to last st, K1.
Row 2: P1, ★ K1, P1, rep from ★ to end.
These 2 rows form 1x1 rib.
Work 2 rows more in rib, dec 2 sts evenly across last of these rows and ending with RS facing for next row.
67 [75: 83: 91: 101] sts.
Change to 7mm (USA 10½) needles.
Beg with a K row cont in st st shaping sides by dec 1 st at each end of 7th row, then 3 foll 6th rows. 59 [67: 75: 83: 93] sts.
Work 9 rows straight.
Inc 1 st at each end of next and 3 foll 4th rows.
67 [75: 83: 91: 101] sts.
Cont straight until back meas 33 [34: 35: 36: 37]cm, ending with RS facing for next row.
Shape armholes
Cast off 5 [7: 7: 8: 9] sts at beg of next 2 rows.
57 [61: 69: 75: 83] sts.
Dec 1 st at each end of next 3 rows, then foll 1 [2: 3: 4: 5] alt rows. 49 [51: 57: 61: 67] sts. ★★
Cont straight until armholes meas 21 [22: 23: 24: 25] cm, ending with RS facing for next row.
Shape shoulders
Next row (RS): Cast off 5 [5: 6: 7: 8] sts, K until there are 8 [9: 10: 11: 12] sts on right hand needle, turn and work this

side first.
Next row: Cast off 3 sts, P to end.
Cast off rem 5 [6: 7: 8: 9] sts.
With RS facing rejoin yarn to rem sts, cast off centre 23 [23: 25: 25: 27] sts, K to end.
Complete to match first side reversing shapings.

FRONT
Work as given for back to ★★.
Cont straight until 10 [10: 12: 12: 14] rows less have been worked than on back to shape shoulders, ending with **WS** facing for next row.
Divide for neck
Next row (RS): K16 [17: 20: 22: 25], turn and leave rem sts on a stitch holder.
Next row: Purl.
Dec 1 st at neck edge of next 5 rows, then foll 1 [1: 2: 2: 3] foll alt rows.
Work 1 row, ending with RS facing for next row.
Shape shoulder
Next row (RS): Cast off 5 [5: 6: 7: 8] sts, K to end.
Work 1 row.
Cast off rem 5 [6: 7: 8: 9] sts.
With RS facing rejoin yarn to rem sts, cast off centre 17 sts, K to end.
Complete to match first side reversing shapings.

SLEEVES

Using 6mm (USA 10) needles cast on 31 [33: 33: 33: 35] sts.

Work 4 rows in 1x1 rib as given for back, ending with RS facing for next row.

Change to 7mm (USA 10½) needles.

Beg with a K row cont in st st shaping sides by inc 1 st at each end of 5th row, then every foll 6th row to 39 [39: 37: 37: 39] sts, then every foll 8th row to 51 [53: 53: 53: 55] sts.

Cont straight until sleeve meas 47 [48: 49: 49: 49] cm, ending with RS facing for next row.

Shape top

Cast off 5 [7: 7: 8: 9] sts at beg of next 2 rows.

41 [39: 39: 37: 37] sts.

Dec 1 st at each end of next 5 [1: 1: 1: 1] rows, then 3 [5: 7: 9: 10] foll alt rows, then every row to 19 [17: 17: 15: 13] sts.

Cast off 6 [5: 5: 4: 3] sts at beg of next 2 rows.

Cast off rem 7 sts.

MAKING UP

Press as described on the information page.

Join both shoulder seams using back stitch or mattress stitch if preferred.

Collar

With RS facing using 6mm (USA 10½) circular needle beg and ending at left shoulder seam, pick up and knit 15 [15: 16: 16: 19] sts down left side of neck, 17 sts from front, 15 [15: 16: 16: 19] sts up right side of neck and 29 [29: 31: 31: 33] sts from back.

76 [76: 80: 80: 88] sts.

Working in rounds, beg with a P round cont in st st until collar meas 13cm.

Change to 7mm (USA 10½) circular needle.

Cont until collar meas 18cm from pick up round.

Next round: ★ K1, P1, rep from ★ to end.

Work 4 more rounds. Cast off in rib.

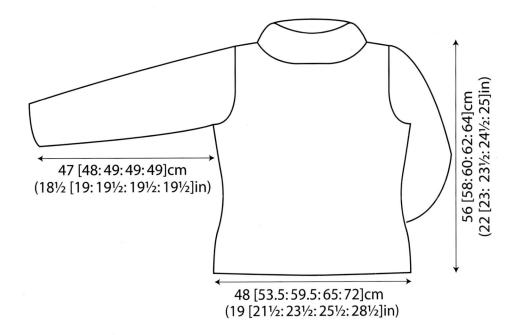

47 [48: 49: 49: 49]cm
(18½ [19: 19½: 19½: 19½]in)

56 [58: 60: 62: 64]cm
(22 [23: 23½: 24½: 25]in)

48 [53.5: 59.5: 65: 72]cm
(19 [21½: 23½: 25½: 28½]in)

Grace

SIZE

	S	M	L	XL	XXL	
To fit bust						
	81-86	91-96	102-107	112-117	122-127	cm
	32-34	36-38	40-42	44-46	48-50	in

YARN

Rowan Colourscape

7	8	8	9	10	x 100gm

(photographed in 436 Northern Lights)

NEEDLES

1 pair 7mm (no 2) (USA 10½) needles
Stitch holder

TENSION

14 sts and 18 rows to 10cm measured over st st using 7mm (no 2) (USA 10½) needles.

BACK (knitted from back to front in 1 piece)
Using 7mm (USA 10½) needles cast on 154 [164: 176: 188: 198] sts.
Row 1 (RS): K1, (K1, P1) twice, K to last 5 sts, (P1, K1) twice, K1.
Row 2: K1, (P1, K1) twice, P to last 5 sts, (K1, P1) twice, K1.
These 2 rows form patt.
Cont in patt until work meas 72 [74: 76: 78: 80]cm, ending with RS facing for next row.
Divide for neck
Next row (RS): Patt 64 [69: 74: 80: 84], turn and leave rem sts on a stitch holder.
Work right and left front separately.

RIGHT FRONT
Next row (WS): K1, (P1, K1) twice, P to last 5 sts, (K1, P1) twice, K1.
This row sets patt, cont in patt as follows-
Work 6 rows more, ending with RS facing for next row.
Next row (RS): K1, (K1, P1) twice, K to last 6 sts, inc in next st, (P1, K1) twice, K1.65 [70: 75: 81: 85] sts.
Cont in patt shaping sides by inc 1 st as before at end of every foll 8th row to 69 [72: 81: 85: 92] sts, then every foll 10th row to 77 [82: 88: 94: 99] sts, working inc sts in st st.
Cont straight until same number of rows have been worked as on back.

Cast off in patt.
With RS facing rejoin yarn to rem sts, cast off centre 26 [26: 28: 28: 30] sts (1 st now on right needle), (K1, P1) twice, K to last 5 sts, (P1, K1) twice, K1.
Complete to match first side reversing shapings.

MAKING UP
Press as described on the information page.

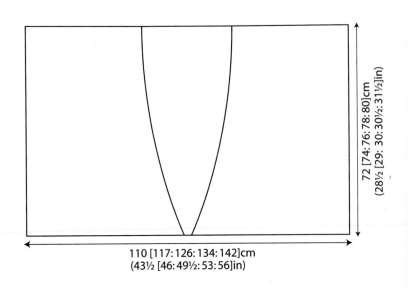

72 [74: 76: 78: 80]cm
(28½ [29: 30: 30½: 31½]in)

110 [117: 126: 134: 142]cm
(43½ [46: 49½: 53: 56]in)

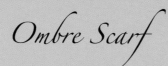

Ombre Scarf

YARN
Rowan Colourscape
2 x 100gm (photographed in 431 Cherry)

NEEDLES
1 pair 7mm (no 2) (USA 10½) needles

TENSION
14 sts and 18 rows to 10cm measured over st st on 7mm (no 2)
(USA 10½) needles

Using 7mm (USA 10½) needles cast on 22 sts.
Knit 4 rows.
Row 1 (RS). K into front and back of 1st st, knit to last 2
sts, k2tog.
Row 2. Purl.
These 2 rows set patt.
Cont in patt until scarf meas 180cm, ending with WS facing
for next row.
Knit 2 rows.
Cast off knitways on WS.

MAKING UP
Press as described on the information page.

Jinx

SIZE

	S	M	L	XL	XXL	
To fit bust						
	81–86	91–96	102–107	112–117	122–127	cm
	32–34	36–38	40–42	44–46	48–50	in

YARN

Rowan Colourscape

5	6	7	7	8	x 100gm

(photographed in Frosty 433)

NEEDLES

1 pair 7mm (no 2) (USA 10½) needles
1 pair 6mm (no 4) (USA 10) needles
Stitch holder

TENSION

14 sts and 18 rows to 10cm measured over st st using 7mm (no 2) (USA 10½) needles.

BACK
Using 6mm (USA 10) needles cast on 66 [72: 82: 90: 100] sts.
Work 4 rows in garter st ending with RS facing for next row.
Change to 7mm (USA 10½) needles.
Beg with a K row cont in st st until back meas 31 [32: 33: 34: 35] cm, ending with RS facing for next row.
Shape armhole
Cast off 4 [5: 6: 6: 6] sts at beg of next 2 rows. 58 [62: 70: 78: 88] sts.
Dec 1 st at each end of next 3 [3: 5: 7: 9] rows, then on foll 1 [2: 1: 1: 1] alt rows. 50 [52: 58: 62: 68] sts.
Cont straight until armholes meas 21 [22: 23: 24: 25] cm, ending with RS facing for next row.
Shape shoulders
Next row (RS): Cast off 5 [5: 6: 7: 8] sts, K until there are 8 [9: 10: 11: 12] sts on right needle, turn and leave rem sts on a stitch holder.
Work each side of neck separately.
Next row: Cast off 3 sts, P to end.
Cast off rem 5 [6: 7: 8: 9] sts.
With RS facing rejoin yarn to rem sts, cast off centre 24 [24: 26: 26: 28] sts,
K to end.
Complete to match first side reversing shaping

LEFT FRONT
Using 6mm needles cast on 42 [45: 50: 54: 59] sts.

Work 4 rows in garter st ending with RS facing for next row.
Change to 7mm (USA 10½) needles.
Next row (RS): K to last 17 sts, turn and leave these 17 sts on a stitch holder.
Beg with a P row, cont in st st on rem 25 [28: 33: 37: 42] sts until left front matches back to shape armholes, ending with RS facing for next row.
Shape armhole
Next row (RS): Cast off 4 [5: 6: 6: 6] sts, K to end.
21 [23: 27: 31: 36] sts.
Work 1 row.
Dec 1 st at beg of next 3 [3: 5: 7: 9] rows, then on foll 1 [2: 1: 1: 1] alt rows. 17 [18: 21: 23: 26] sts.
Cont straight until 28 [28: 30: 30: 32] rows less have been worked than on back to shape shoulders.
Shape neck
Dec 1 st at end of next row, then foll alt row, then every foll 4th row to 10 [11: 13: 15: 17] sts.
Work 5 [5: 3: 3: 1] rows.
Shape shoulder
Next row (RS): Cast off 5 [5: 6: 7: 8] sts, P to end.
Work 1 row.
Cast off rem 5 [6: 7: 8: 9] sts.

RIGHT FRONT
Using 6mm needles cast on 42 [45: 50: 54: 59] sts.

Work 4 rows in garter st ending with RS facing for next row.

Next row (RS): K17 and leave these 17 sts on a stitch holder. Change to 7mm (USA 10½) needles and K to end.

Cont in st st until right front matches back to shape armholes, ending with **WS** facing for next row.

Complete to match left front reversing shapings

SLEEVES

Using 6mm (USA 10) needles cast on 30 [32: 34: 34: 36] sts.

Cont in garter st until sleeve meas 12cm, ending with RS facing for next row.

Change to 7mm (USA 10½) needles.

Beg with a K row cont in st st shaping sides by inc 1 st at each end of 5th row, then every foll 6th row to 44 [44: 44: 44: 46] sts, then every foll 8th row to 50 [52: 54: 54: 56] sts.

Cont straight until sleeve meas 53 [54: 55: 55: 55] cm, ending with RS facing for next row.

Shape top

Cast off 4 [5: 6: 6: 6] sts at beg of next 2 rows.

42 [42: 42: 42: 44] sts.

Dec 1 st at each end of next row, then foll 2 [4: 6: 8: 9] alt rows, then every row to 18 sts.

Cast off 6 sts at beg of next 2 rows.

Cast off rem 6 sts.

MAKING UP

Press as described on the information page.

Join side, shoulder and sleeve seams using back stitch or mattress stitch if preferred.

Left front edging

With RS facing, using 6mm (USA 10) needles, rejoin yarn to 17 sts left on a stitch holder at left front edge.

Cont in garter st until edging matches left front to first neck dec when slightly stretched, ending with RS facing for next row.

Inc 1 st at beg of next row and at same edge on foll 7 alt rows, working inc sts in garter st.

25 sts.

Cont straight until edging is long enough when slightly stretched to reach centre back neck, ending with RS facing for next row.

Cast off.

Right front edging

With **WS** facing using 6mm (USA 10) needles rejoin yarn to 17 sts left on a stitch holder at right front edge.

Complete as given for left front edging reversing shaping.

Sew cast off edges of left and right front edgings at centre back and slip stitch in position around neck.

Turn back first 6cm of sleeve to from cuffs.

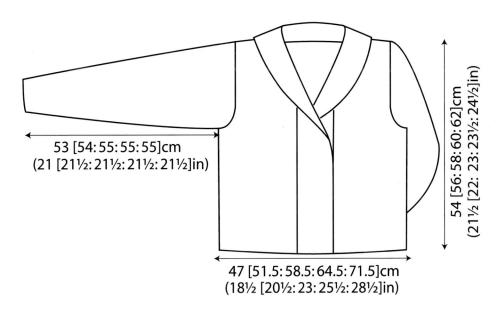

53 [54: 55: 55: 55]cm
(21 [21½: 21½: 21½: 21½]in)

47 [51.5: 58.5: 64.5: 71.5]cm
(18½ [20½: 23: 25½: 28½]in)

54 [56: 58: 60: 62]cm
(21½ [22: 23: 23½: 24½]in)

Sigh

SIZE

	S	M	L	XL	XXL	
To fit bust						
	81–86	91–96	102–107	112–117	122–127	cm
	32–34	36–38	40–42	44–46	48–50	in

YARN

Rowan Colourscape

	S	M	L	XL	XXL	
	5	6	7	7	8	x 100gm

(photographed in 433 Frosty)

NEEDLES

1 pair 7mm (no 2) (USA 10½) needles
1 pair 6mm (no 4) (USA 10) needles
7mm (no 2) (USA 10½) circular needle
6mm (no 4) (USA 10) circular needle
Cable needle
Stitch holder

TENSION

14 sts and 18 rows to 10cm measured over st st using 7mm (no 2) (USA 10½) needles.

SPECIAL ABBREVIATION

C16B=slip next 8 sts onto cable needle and hold at back of work, K8, then K8 from cable needle

BACK

Using 6mm (USA 10) needles cast on 70 [78: 86: 94: 106] sts.
Row 1 (RS): ★ K2, P2, rep from ★ to last 2 sts, K2.
Row 2: P2, ★ K2, P2, rep from ★ to end.
These 2 rows form 2x2 rib.
Work 2 rows more in rib, dec 0 [2: 0: 0: 2] sts evenly across last of these rows and ending with RS facing for next row.
70 [76: 86: 94: 104] sts.
Change to 7mm (USA 10½) needles. ★★
Beg with a K row cont in st st until back meas 36 [37: 38: 39: 40] cm, ending with RS facing for next row.

Shape armholes
Cast off 5 [7: 7: 8: 9] sts at beg of next 2 rows.
60 [62: 72: 78: 86] sts.
Dec 1 st at each end of next 3 [3: 5: 7: 7] rows, then foll 2 [2: 2: 1: 3] alt rows. 50 [52: 58: 62: 66] sts.
Cont straight until armholes meas 21 [22: 23: 24: 25] cm, ending with RS facing for next row.

Shape shoulders
Next row (RS): Cast off 5 [6: 7: 8: 8] sts, K until there are 9 [9: 10: 11: 12] sts on right hand needle, turn and work this side first.

Next row: Cast off 3 sts, P to end.
Cast off rem 6 [6: 7: 8: 9] sts.
With RS facing rejoin yarn to rem sts, cast off centre 22 [22: 24: 24: 26] sts, K to end.
Complete to match first side reversing shapings.

FRONT

Work as given for back to ★★.
Row 1 (RS): K25 [28: 33: 37: 42], P2, K16, P2, K to end.
Row 2 and every foll alt row: P25 [28: 33: 37: 42], K2, P16, K2, P to end.
Rows 3 to 10: rep rows 1 and 2.
Row 11: K25 [28: 33: 37: 42], P2, C16B, P2, K to end.
Rows 13 to 20: As rows 1 and 2.
These 20 rows form patt.
Cont in patt until front matches back to shape armholes, ending with RS facing for next row.

Shape armholes
Keeping patt correct, cast off 5 [7: 7: 8: 9] sts at beg of next 2 rows. 60 [62: 72: 78: 86] sts.
Dec 1 st at each end of next 3 [3: 5: 7: 7] rows, then foll 2 [2: 2: 1: 3] alt rows. 50 [52: 58: 62: 66] sts.
Cont straight in patt until 10 [10: 12: 12: 14] rows less have been worked than on back to shape shoulders.

Divide for neck
Next row (RS): Patt 17 [18: 21: 23: 25], turn and leave rem sts

on a stitch holder.

Work each side of neck separately.

Work 1 row.

Dec 1 st at neck edge in next 5 rows, then foll 1 [1: 2: 2: 3] alt rows.

Work 1 row.

Shape shoulder

Next row (RS): Cast off 5 [6: 7: 8: 8] sts, patt to end.

Work 1 row.

Cast off rem 6 [6: 7: 8: 9] sts.

With RS facing rejoin yarn to rem sts, cast off centre 16 sts, patt to end.

Complete to match first side reversing shapings.

SLEEVES

Using 6mm (USA 10) needles cast on 34 [34: 34: 34: 38] sts.

Work 4 rows in 2x2 rib as given for back dec 3 [1: 1: 1: 3] sts evenly across last of these rows and ending with RS facing for next row. 31 [33: 33: 33: 35] sts.

Change to 7mm (USA 10½) needles.

Beg with a K row cont in st st shaping sides by inc 1 st at each end of 5th row, then every foll 6th row to 39 [39: 37: 37: 39] sts, then every foll 8th row to 51 [53: 53: 53: 55] sts.

Cont straight until sleeve meas 47 [48: 49: 49: 49] cm, ending with RS facing for next row.

Shape top

Cast off 5 [7: 7: 8: 9] sts at beg of next 2 rows.

41 [39: 39: 37: 37] sts.

Dec 1 st at each end of next 5 [1: 1: 1: 1] rows, then 3 [5: 7: 9: 10] foll alt rows, then every row to 19 [17: 17: 15: 13] sts.

Cast off 6 [5: 5: 4: 3] sts at beg of next 2 rows.

Cast off rem 7 sts.

MAKING UP

Press as described on the information page.

Join both shoulder seams using back stitch or mattress stitch if preferred.

Collar

With RS facing using 6mm (USA 10½) circular needle beg and ending at left shoulder seam, pick up and knit 15 [15: 16: 16: 19] sts down left side of neck, 17 sts from front, 15 [15: 16: 16: 19] sts up right side of neck and 29 [29: 31: 31: 33] sts from back.

76 [76: 80: 80: 88] sts.

Working in rounds, beg with a P round cont in st st until collar meas 13cm.

Change to 7mm (USA 10½) circular needle.

Cont until collar meas 18cm from pick up round.

Next round: ★ K2, P2, rep from ★ to end.

Work 4 more rounds. Cast off in rib.

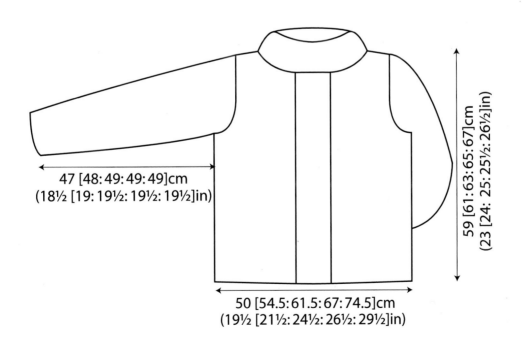

47 [48: 49: 49: 49]cm
(18½ [19: 19½: 19½: 19½]in)

59 [61: 63: 65: 67]cm
(23 [24: 25: 25½: 26½]in)

50 [54.5: 61.5: 67: 74.5]cm
(19½ [21½: 24½: 26½: 29½]in)

Smoulder

SIZE

	S	M	L	XL	XXL	
To fit bust						
	81-86	91-96	102-107	112-117	122-127	cm
	32-34	36-38	40-42	44-46	48-50	in

YARN

Rowan Colourscape

5	6	7	7	8	x 100gm

(photographed in Northern Lights 436)

NEEDLES

1 pair 7mm (no 2) (USA 10½) needles
1 pair 6mm (USA 10) needles
Stitch holder

TENSION

14 sts and 18 rows to 10cm measured over st st using 7mm (no 2) (USA 10½) needles.

BACK

Using 6mm (USA 10) needles cast on 75 [83: 91: 99: 109] sts.
Work 2 rows in garter st, ending with RS facing for next row.
Change to 7mm (USA 10½) needles.
Beg with a K row cont in st st shaping sides by dec 1 st at each end of 5th [7th: 9th: 11th: 13th] row, then 5 foll 6th rows, then 2 foll 4th rows.
59 [67: 75: 83: 93] sts.
Work 1 row, ending with RS facing for next row.
Next row (RS): ★ K1, P1, rep from ★ to last st, K1.
Next row: P1, ★ K1, P1, rep from ★ to end.
These 2 rows form 1x1 rib.
Work 8 rows more in rib, ending with RS facing for next row.
Beg with a K row, cont in st st shaping sides by inc 1 st at each end of 3rd row, then 3 foll 6th rows. 67 [75: 83: 91: 101] sts.
Work 5 rows more, ending with RS facing for next row. (Back should meas 45.5 [46.5: 47.5: 48.5: 50] cm).
Shape armholes
Cast off 4 [6: 6: 6: 6] sts at beg of next 2 rows.
59 [63: 71: 79: 89] sts.
Dec 1 st at each end of next 3 [3: 5: 7: 9] rows, then foll 2 alt rows. 49 [53: 57: 61: 67] sts.
Cont straight until armholes meas 21 [22: 23: 24: 25] cm, ending with RS facing for next row.
Shape shoulders
Next row (RS): Cast off 4 [5: 6: 7: 8] sts, K until there are

8 [9: 9: 10: 11] sts on right needle, turn and leave rem sts on a stitch holder.
Work each side of neck separately.
Next row: Cast off 3 sts, P to end.
Cast off rem 5 [6: 6: 7: 8] sts.
With RS facing rejoin yarn to rem sts, cast off centre 25 [25: 27: 27: 29] sts, P to end.
Complete to match first side reversing shaping

LEFT FRONT

Using 6mm (USA 10) needles cast on 33 [37: 41: 45: 50] sts.
Work 2 rows in garter st, ending with RS facing for next row.
Change to 7mm (USA 10½) needles.
Beg with a K row, cont in st st shaping side by dec 1 st at beg of 5th [7th: 9th: 11th: 13th] row, then 5 foll 6th rows, then 2 foll 4th rows.
25 [29: 33: 37: 42] sts.
Work 1 row, ending with RS facing for next row.
Next row (RS): ★ K1, P1, rep from ★ to last 2 [1: 1: 1: 1] sts, K1, P1 [0: 0: 0: 0].
Next row: K1 [0: 0: 0: 0], P1, ★ K1, P1, rep from ★ to end.
These 2 rows form rib.
Work 8 rows more in rib, ending with RS facing for next row.
Shape neck
Cont in st st shaping side and neck by inc 1 st at beg **and at same time** dec 1 st at end of 3rd row, then 3 foll 6th rows.

Work 5 rows straight, ending with RS facing for next row.

Shape armhole

Next row (RS): Cast off 4 [6: 6: 6: 6] sts, K to last 2 sts, K2tog. 20 [22: 26: 30: 35] sts.

Work 1 row.

Dec 1 st at beg of next 3 [3: 5: 7: 9] rows, then on foll 2 alt rows **and at same time** dec 1 st at neck edge in 5th row, then 0 [0: 0: 1: 1] foll 6th row. 14 [16: 18: 19: 22] sts.

Dec 1 st at neck edge only on 4th [4th: 2nd: 6th : 4th] and every foll 6th row to 9 [11: 12: 14: 16] sts.

Cont straight until left front matches back to shape shoulders, ending with RS facing for next row.

Shape shoulder

Next row (RS): Cast off 4 [5: 6: 7: 8] sts, patt to end.

Work 1 row.

Cast off rem 5 [6: 6: 7: 8] sts.

RIGHT FRONT

Using 6mm (USA 10) needles cast on 33 [37: 41: 45: 50] sts.

Work 2 rows in garter st, ending with RS facing for next row.

Change to 7mm (USA 10½) needles.

Beg with a K row, cont in st st shaping side by dec 1 st at end of 5th [7th: 9th: 11th: 13th] row, then 5 foll 6th rows, then 2 foll 4throws. 25 [29: 33: 37: 42] sts.

Work 1 row, ending with RS facing for next row.

Next row (RS): P1 [0: 0: 0: 0].★ K1, P1, rep from ★ to last st, K1.

Next row: P1, ★ K1, P1, rep from ★ to last 2 [1: 1: 1: 1] sts, K1, P1 [0: 0: 0: 0].

These 2 rows form rib.

Work 8 rows more in rib, ending with RS facing for next row.

Complete as given for left front reversing shapings.

SLEEVES (BOTH ALIKE)

Using 6mm (USA 10) needles cast on 31 [33: 33: 33: 35] sts.

Row 1 (RS): ★ K1, P1, rep from ★ to last st, K1.

Row 2: P1, ★ K1, P1, rep from ★ to end.

Row 3: As row 2.

Row 4: As row 1.

These 4 rows form patt.

Work 8 rows more in patt.

Change to 7mm (USA 10½) needles.

Beg with a K row, cont in st st shaping sides by inc 1 st at each end of 3rd row, then every foll 6th row to 45 [45: 43: 43: 45] sts, then every foll 8th row to 51 [53: 53: 53: 55] sts.

Cont straight until sleeve meas 47 [48: 49: 49: 49] cm, ending with RS facing for next row.

Shape top

Cast off 4 [6: 6: 6: 6] sts at beg of next 2 rows.

43 [41: 41: 41: 43] sts.

Dec 1 st at each end of next 6 [3: 1: 1:1] rows, then 1 [4: 6: 8: 9] foll alt rows, then every row to 17 sts.

Cast off 5 sts at beg of next 2 rows. Cast off rem 7 sts.

MAKING UP

Press as described on the information page.

Join side and shoulder seams using back stitch or mattress stitch if preferred.

Front edging

With RS facing, using 6mm (USA 10) needles cast on 11 sts.

Cont in patt as given for sleeves until front band is long enough when slightly stretched to fit up left front, around neck and down right front, beg and ending at bottom edges, ending with RS facing for next row.

Cast off. Slip stitch in position.

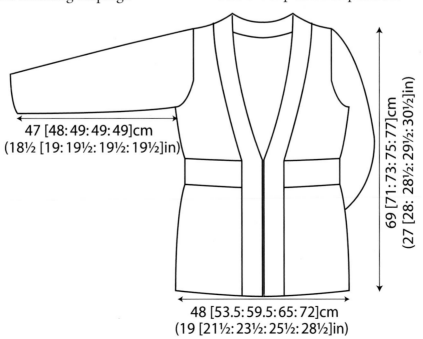

47 [48: 49: 49: 49]cm
(18½ [19: 19½: 19½: 19½]in)

69 [71: 73: 75: 77]cm
(27 [28: 28½: 29½: 30½]in)

48 [53.5: 59.5: 65: 72]cm
(19 [21½: 23½: 25½: 28½]in)

Solace

⬤ ⬤

SIZE

	S	M	L	XL	XXL	
To fit bust						
	81–86	91–96	102–107	112–117	122–127	cm
	32–34	36–38	40–42	44–46	48–50	in

YARN

Rowan Colourscape

4	5	5	6	6	x 100gm

(photographed in 435 Ghost)

NEEDLES

1 pair 7mm (no 2) (USA 10½) needles
7mm (no 2) (USA 10½) circular needle
Stitch holder

TENSION

14 sts and 18 rows to 10cm measured over st st using 7mm (no 2) (USA 10½) needles.

BOTTOM PANEL

Using 7mm (USA 10½) circular needle cast on 144 [160: 176: 192: 208] sts.

Beg with a K row and working in rows, work 12 rows in st st, ending with RS facing for next row.

Next row (RS): K34 [38: 42: 46: 50], K2tog, Sl 1, K1, psso, K68 [76: 84: 92: 100], K2tog, Sl 1, K1, psso, K to end. 140 [156: 172: 188: 204] sts.

Work 11 rows straight, ending with RS facing for next row.

Next row (RS): K33 [37: 41: 45: 49], K2tog, Sl 1, K1, psso, K66 [74: 82: 90: 98], K2tog, Sl 1, K1, psso, K to end. 136 [152: 168: 184: 200] sts.

Cont straight until panel meas 30 [32: 34: 36: 38] cm, ending with RS facing for next row. Cast off.

BACK AND FRONT YOKE (knitted in 1 piece beg at right sleeve)

Using 7mm (USA 10½) needles cast on 50 [52: 54: 54: 56] sts.

Beg with a K row cont in st st shaping sides by inc 1 st at each end of 15th row, then foll 14th [16th: 16th: 18th: 18th] row. 54 [56: 58: 58: 60] sts.

Work 17 rows straight, ending with RS facing for next row. Place markers at each end of last row to denote top of right sleeve.

Work 26 [30: 36: 40: 44] rows more, ending with RS facing for next row.

Work should meas 40 [43: 47: 50: 52] cm.

Divide for neck and right front

Next row (RS): K27 [28: 29: 29: 30] turn and leave rem sts on a stitch holder.

Cast off 3 sts at beg of next row and at same edge of foll 7 [7: 8: 8: 8] alt rows, ending with RS facing for next row.

Cast off rem 3 [4: 2: 2: 3] sts.

Back

With RS facing rejoin yarn to rem sts, K2tog, K to end. 26 [27: 28: 28: 29] sts.

Dec 1 st at end of next row and at same edge on foll 2 rows. 23 [24: 25: 25: 26] sts.

Work 26 [26: 28: 28: 30] rows straight, ending with RS facing for next row.

Inc 1 st at beg of 1st row and at same edge of next 2 rows.

Leave these 26 [27: 28: 28: 29] sts on a stitch holder.

Left front

Using 7mm (USA 10½) needles cast on 3 [4: 2: 2: 3] sts.

Beg with a K row, cont in st st cast on 3 sts at beg of 2nd row and at same edge of foll 7 [7: 8: 8: 8] alt rows, ending with RS facing for next row. 27 [28: 29: 29: 30] sts.

Next row (RS): K27 [28: 29: 29: 30], then working on 26 [27: 28: 28: 29] sts left on a stitch holder, inc in next st, K to end. 54 [56: 58: 58: 60] sts.

Beg with a P row work 25 [29: 35: 39: 43] rows in st st, ending with RS facing for next row. (Work should meas 73 [79: 87: 92: 95] cm)

Place markers at each end of last row to denote top of left sleeve.

Work 16 rows more, ending with RS facing for next row Cont shaping sides by dec 1 st at each end of next and foll 14th [16th: 16th: 18th: 18th] row. 50 [52: 54: 56: 58] sts.

Work 14 rows straight. Cast off.

MAKING UP

Press as described on the information page.

Join sleeve seams from cast on edge to first set of markers and from cast off edge to second set of markers.

Join bottom panel to back and front yokes, matching front edges.

Front edging

With RS facing using 7mm (USA 10½) circular needle, pick up and knit 43 [45: 47: 49: 51] sts up right front edge of bottom panel, 27 [28: 29: 29: 30] sts up shaped edge of yoke, 34 [34: 36: 36: 38] sts from back of neck, 27 [28: 29: 29: 30] sts down shaped edge of yoke and 43 [45: 47: 49: 51] sts down left front edge of bottom panel.

174 [180: 188: 192: 200] sts.

Beg with a K row, work 3 rows in reversed st st.

Next row: (Buttonhole row) P43 [46: 48: 51: 54], cast off 2 sts (2 sts to be cast on over these 2 sts on next row) P to end.

Work 2 rows more in reversed st st. Cast off.

Sew on button.

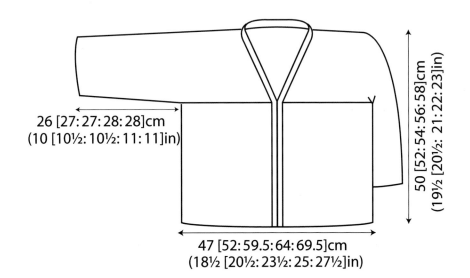

26 [27: 27: 28: 28]cm
(10 [10½: 10½: 11: 11]in)

50 [52: 54: 56: 58]cm
(19½ [20½: 21: 22: 23]in)

47 [52: 59.5: 64: 69.5]cm
(18½ [20½: 23½: 25: 27½]in)

Tempo

SIZE

	S	M	L	XL	XXL	
To fit bust						
	81–86	91–96	102–107	112–117	122–127	cm
	32–34	36–38	40–42	44–46	48–50	in

YARN

Rowan Colourscape

4	5	5	6	7	x 100gm

(photographed in 430 Carnival)

NEEDLES

1 pair 7mm (no 2) (USA 10½) needles
1 pair 6mm (no 4) (USA 10) needles
Stitch holder

TENSION

14 sts and 18 rows to 10cm measured over st st using 7mm (no 2) (USA 10½) needles.

BACK

Using 6mm (USA 10) needles cast on 72 [78: 88: 96: 106] sts.
Work 4 rows in garter st, ending with RS facing for next row.
Change to 7mm (USA 10½) needles.
Beg with a K row cont in st st shaping sides by dec 1 st at each end of 17th row, then 2 foll 20th rows. 66 [72: 82: 90: 100] sts.
Cont straight until back meas 50 [51: 52: 53: 54] cm, ending with RS facing for next row.

Shape armholes

Cast off 4 [5: 7: 9: 10] sts at beg of next 2 rows.
58 [62: 68: 72: 80] sts.
Next row (RS): P1, K3, Sl 1, K1, psso, K to last 6 sts, K2tog, K3, P1.
Next row: K1, P3, P2tog, P to last 6 sts, P2togtbl, P3, K1.
54 [58: 64: 68: 76] sts.
Working all decs as set in these 2 rows dec 1 st at each end of next 3 rows, then foll 1 [1: 2: 2: 3] alt rows.
46 [50: 54: 58: 64] sts.
Cont straight in st st with edge st in reversed st st until armholes meas 21 [22: 23: 24: 25] cm, ending with RS facing for next row.

Shape shoulders

Next row (RS): Cast off 4 [5: 6: 7: 8] sts, K until there are 8 [9: 9: 10: 11] sts on right needle, turn and leave rem sts on a stitch holder.
Work each side of neck separately.

Next row: Cast off 3 sts, P to end.
Cast off rem 5 [6: 6: 7: 8] sts.
With RS facing rejoin yarn to rem sts, cast off centre 22 [22: 24: 24: 26] sts, P to end.
Complete to match first side reversing shaping

POCKET LININGS (MAKE 2)

Using 7mm (USA 10½) needles cast on 15 sts.
Beg with a K row, cont in st st until pocket lining meas 15cm, ending with **WS** facing for next row.
Leave these 15 sts on a stitch holder.

LEFT FRONT

Using 6mm (USA 10) needles cast on 45 [48: 53: 57: 62] sts.
Work 4 rows in garter st, ending with RS facing for next row.
Change to 7mm (USA 10½) needles.
Row 1 (RS): K to last 13 sts, P1, K7, P5.
Row 2: K5, P7, K1, P to end.
These 2 rows form patt.
Con in patt shaping sides by dec 1 st at beg of 15th row, then foll 20th row. 43 [46: 51: 55: 60] sts.
Work 9 rows more, ending with RS facing for next row.

Divide for pocket

Next row (RS): Patt 13 [16: 21: 25: 30], cast off 15 sts, patt to end.
Next row: Patt 15, with **WS** facing patt across 15 sts left on a

stitch holder for pocket lining, patt to end.

Dec 1 st at beg of foll 9th row. 42 [45: 50: 54: 59] sts.

Cont straight in patt until left front matches back shape armholes, ending with RS facing for next row.

Shape armhole

Next row (RS): Cast off 4 [5: 7: 9: 10] sts, patt to end. 38 [40: 43: 45: 49] sts.

Work 1 row.

Next row: P1, K3, Sl 1, K1, psso, K to last 15 sts, K2tog, patt to end. 36 [38: 41: 43: 47] sts.

Next row: Patt to last 6 sts, P2togtbl, P3, K1. 35 [37: 40: 42: 46] sts.

These 2 rows set armhole and neck shaping.

Dec 1 st at armhole edge as set in next 3 rows, then on foll alt row **at same time** dec 1 st at neck edge as set in next and 2 foll alt rows. 28 [30: 33: 35: 39] sts.

Dec1 st at neck edge only in next and every foll 4th row to 22 [24: 25: 27: 29] sts.

Cont straight until left front matches back to shoulder shaping, ending with RS facing for next row.

Shape shoulder

Next row (RS): Cast off 4 [5: 6: 7: 8] sts, patt to end. 18 [20: 21: 23: 25] sts.

Work 1 row.

Cast off 5 [6: 6: 7: 8] sts, patt to end.

Do not break off yarn and leave rem 13 sts on a stitch holder.

RIGHT FRONT

Using 6mm (USA 10) needles cast on 45 [48: 53: 57: 62] sts.

Work 4 rows in garter st, ending with RS facing for next row.

Change to 7mm (USA 10½) needles.

Row 1 (RS): P5, K7, P1, K to end.

Row 2: P to last 13 sts, K1, P7, K5.

These 2 rows form patt.

Cont in patt shaping sides by dec 1 st at end of 15th row, then foll 20th row. 43 [46: 51: 55: 60] sts.

Work 9 rows more, ending with RS facing for next row.

Divide for pocket

Next row (RS): Patt 15, cast off 15 sts, patt to end.

Next row: Patt 13 [16: 21: 25: 30], with **WS** facing patt across 15 sts left on a stitch holder for pocket lining, patt to end.

Dec1 st at end of 9th row. 42 [45: 50: 54: 59] sts.

Cont straight until right front matches back to armhole shaping, ending with **WS** facing for next row.

Shape armhole

Next row (WS): Cast off 4 [5: 7: 9: 10] sts, patt to end. 38 [40: 43: 45: 49] sts.

Next row: Patt 13, Sl 1, K1, psso, patt to last 6 sts, K2tog, K3, P1. 36 [38: 41: 43: 47] sts.

Next row: K1, P3, P2tog, patt to end. 35 [37: 40: 42: 46] sts.

These 2 rows set armhole and neck shaping.

Complete to match first side reversing shapings

MAKING UP

Press as described on the information page.

Join side and shoulder seams using back stitch or mattress stitch if preferred.

Slip stitch pocket linings to inside of garment.

Left back neck edging

With **WS** facing rejoin yarn to 13 sts left on a stitch holder and cont in st st until edging fits across back neck to centre point, sewing in position at same time, ending with RS facing for next row. Cast off. Join centre back seam.

Right back neck edging

With RS facing rejoin yarn to 13 sts left on a stitch holder and cont in st st until edging fits across back neck to centre point, sewing in position at same time, ending with RS facing for next row. Cast off. Join centre back seam.

Pocket edgings (both alike)

With RS facing, using 6mm (USA 10) needles pick up and knit 15 sts along cast off edge of pocket. Cast off.

Sew ends of pocket edging to garment.

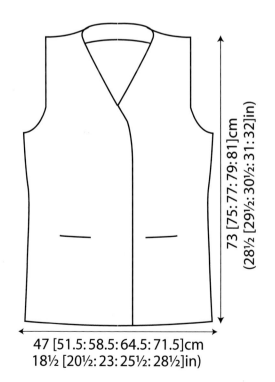

73 [75: 77: 79: 81]cm
(28½ [29½: 30½: 31: 32]in)

47 [51.5: 58.5: 64.5: 71.5]cm
18½ [20½: 23: 25½: 28½]in)

Tender

SIZE

	S	M	L	XL	XXL	
To fit bust						
	81–86	91–96	102–107	112–117	122–127	cm
	32–34	36–38	40–42	44–46	48–50	in

YARN

Rowan Colourscape

	5	6	6	7	7	x 100gm

(photographed in 434 Candy Pink)

NEEDLES

1 pair 7mm (no 2) (USA 10½) needles
1 pair 6mm (no 4) (USA 10) needles
Stitch holders

TENSION

14 sts and 18 rows to 10cm measured over st st using 7mm (no 2) (USA 10½) needles.

MAIN SECTION (knitted in 1 piece beg at right sleeve
Using 6mm (USA 10) needles cast on 106 [110: 110: 114: 118] sts.
Row 1 (RS): ★ K2, P2, rep from ★ to last 2 sts, K2.
Row 2: P2, ★ K2, P2, rep from ★ to end.
These 2 rows form 2x2 rib.
Work 2 rows more in rib dec 2 [2: 0: 0: 2] sts evenly across last of these rows.
104 [108: 110: 114: 116] sts.
Change to 7mm (USA 10½) needles.
Beg with a K row, cont in st st until work meas 41 [44.5: 48.5:

52.5: 56] cm, ending with RS facing for next row.
Divide for neck
Next row (RS): K to centre st, turn and leave rem sts on a stitch holder.
Work front and back separately.

FRONT
Cont straight until front meas 26 [26: 27: 27: 28] cm from divide for neck, ending with RS facing for next row. Place these sts onto a second stitch holder.

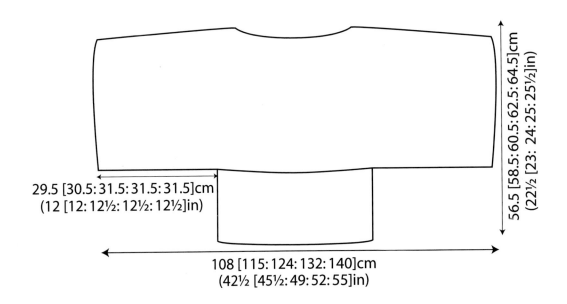

29.5 [30.5: 31.5: 31.5: 31.5]cm
(12 [12: 12½: 12½: 12½]in)

56.5 [58.5: 60.5: 62.5: 64.5]cm
(22½ [23: 24: 25: 25½]in)

108 [115: 124: 132: 140]cm
(42½ [45½: 49: 52: 55]in)

BACK
With RS facing rejoin yarn to rem sts, K2tog, K to end.
Cont on these sts only until same number of rows have been worked as on first side, ending with RS facing for next row.
Break off yarn.

MAIN SECTION
Working across all sts proceed as follows:
Next row (RS): K across all sts on stitch holder for front, inc in first of sts left on stitch holder for back, K to end.
Cont straight until same number of rows have been worked to divide for neck, inc 2 [2: 0: 0: 2] sts evenly across last of these rows and ending with RS facing for next row.
106 [110: 110: 114: 118] sts.
Change to 6mm (USA 10) needles.

Work 4 rows in 2x2 rib. Cast off in rib.

MAKING UP
Press as described on the information page.
Fold in half lengthways and join sleeve seams 29.5 [30.5: 31.5: 31.5: 31.5] cm from cast on and cast off edges using back stitch or mattress stitch if preferred.
Front welt
With RS facing using 6mm (USA 10) needles, pick up and knit 74 [82: 90: 98: 106] sts evenly across bottom edge.
Starting with row 2 of 2x2 rib, work 33 [35: 37: 39: 41] rows in rib.
Cast off in rib.
Back welt
Work as given for front welt.
Join row end edges of welts.

 Valour

SIZE

	S	M	L	XL	XXL	
To fit bust						
	81–86	91–96	102–107	112–117	122–127	cm
	32–34	36–38	40–42	44–46	48–50	in

YARN

Rowan Colourscape

| 4 | 4 | 4 | 5 | 5 | x 100gm |

(photographed in 435 Ghost)

NEEDLES

1 pair 7mm (no 2) (USA 10½) needles
1 pair 6mm (no 4) (USA 10) needles
1 7mm (no 2) crochet hook
1 button

TENSION

14 sts and 18 rows to 10cm measured over st st using 7mm (no 2) (USA 10½) needles.

BACK

Using 7mm (USA 10½) needles cast on 67 [75: 83: 91: 101] sts.
Row 1 (RS): P1 [1: 1: 1: 2], ★ K1, P3, rep from ★ to last 2 [2: 2: 2: 3] sts, K1, P1 [1: 1: 1: 2]
Row 2: K1 [1: 1: 1: 2], ★ P1, K3, rep from ★ to last 2 [2: 2: 2: 3] sts, P1, K1 [1: 1: 1: 2].
These 2 rows form patt.
Cont in patt until back meas 32 [33: 34: 35: 36]cm, ending with RS facing for next row.
Shape armholes
Keeping patt correct, cast off 4 [6: 7: 8: 9] sts at beg of next 2 rows. 59 [63: 69: 75: 83] sts.
Dec 1 st at each end of next 3 rows, then foll 1 [2: 3: 4: 5] alt rows. 51 [53: 57: 61: 67] sts.
Cont straight until armholes meas 22 [23: 24: 25: 26] cm, ending with RS facing for next row.
Shape shoulders
Keeping patt correct cast off 8 [9: 11: 13: 15] sts at beg of next 2 rows.
Work a further 10 rows on rem 35 [35: 35: 35: 37] sts for back collar extension, ending with RS facing for next row.
Cast off.

RIGHT FRONT (knitted sideways beg at front opening edge)
Using 7mm (USA 10½) needles cast on 84 [86: 89: 92: 95] sts.
Row 1 (RS): ★ P3, K1, rep from ★ to last 0 [2: 1: 0: 3] sts, P0 [2: 1: 0: 3].
Row 2: K0 [2: 1: 0: 3], ★ P1, K3, rep from ★ to end.
These 2 rows form patt.
Cont in patt until right front meas 19 [19: 20: 20: 21] cm, ending with RS facing for next row.
Shape collar extension
Keeping patt correct, cast off 8 sts at beg of next row. 76 [78: 81: 84: 87] sts.
Work 9 [11: 13: 17: 17] rows, ending with RS facing for next row. (These rows form shoulder seam section)
Shape armhole
Keeping patt correct, cast off 28 sts at beg of next row. 48 [50: 53: 56: 59] sts.
Dec 1 st at end of next row and at same edge on foll 2 [3: 5: 6: 8] rows. 45 [46: 47: 49: 50] sts.
Work 6 [9: 9: 12: 12] rows, ending with RS facing for next row.
Cast off in patt. (This edge forms side seam)

LEFT FRONT (knitted sideways at beg of front opening edge)
Using 7mm (USA 10½) needles cast on 84 [86: 89: 92: 95] sts.
Row (WS): ★K3, P1, rep from ★ to last 0 [2: 1: 0: 3] sts, K0 [2: 1: 0: 3].
Row 2: ★ P0 [2: 1: 0: 3], ★K1, P3 rep from ★ to end.
These 2 rows form patt.
Complete to match first side reversing shapings by reading WS for RS and vice versa.

MAKING UP

Press as described on the information page.

Join shoulder and collar extension seams using back stitch or mattress stitch if preferred.

Armhole borders (both alike)

With RS facing using 6mm (USA 10) needles pick up and knit 62 [64: 68: 70: 72] sts all round armhole edge.

Cast off knitwise on WS.

Sew on button using photograph as a guide.

Make button loop

Using 7mm crochet hook make length of ch 6cm long. Attach opposite button.

54 [56: 58: 60: 62]cm
(21½ [22: 23: 23½: 24½]in)

48 [53.5: 59.5: 65: 72]cm
19 [21½: 23½: 25½: 28½]in)

Tainted Scarf

YARN
Rowan Colourscape
2 x 100gm (photographed in Frosty 433)

NEEDLES
1 pair 7mm (no 2) (USA 10½) needles

TENSION
14 sts and 18 rows to 10cm measured over st st using 7mm (no 2) (USA 10½) needles.

Using 7mm (USA 10½) needles cast on 24 sts.
Knit 4 rows.
Cont as folls:-
Row 1. K1, (k2tog, k2, knit into front and back of each of next 2 sts, k3, sl, k1, psso) twice, k1.
Row 2. K1, purl to last st, k1.
Rep last 2 rows twice, then row 1 once more.
Rows 8 to 10. Knit.

These 10 rows set patt.
Cont in patt until scarf meas approx. 160cm, ending after row 7 of patt.
Knit 4 rows.
Cast off knitways on WS.

MAKING UP
Press as described on the information page.

sizing guide

Our sizing now conforms to standard clothing sizes. Therefore if you buy a standard size 12 in clothing, then our size 12 or Medium patterns will fit you perfectly.

Dimensions in the charts shown are body measurements, not garment dimensions, therefore please refer to the measuring guide to help you to determine which is the best size for you to knit.

STANDARD SIZING GUIDE FOR WOMEN

UK SIZE	8	10	12	14	16	18	20	22	
USA Size	6	8	10	12	14	16	18	20	
EUR Size	34	36	38	40	42	44	46	48	
To fit bust	32	34	36	38	40	42	44	46	inches
	82	87	92	97	102	107	112	117	cm
To fit waist	24	26	28	30	32	34	36	38	inches
	61	66	71	76	81	86	91	96	cm
To fit hips	34	36	38	40	42	44	46	48	inches
	87	92	97	102	107	112	117	122	cm

CASUAL SIZING GUIDE FOR WOMEN

As there are some designs that are intended to fit more generously, we have introduced our casual sizing guide. The designs that fall into this group can be recognised by the size range: Small, Medium, Large & Xlarge. Each of these sizes cover two sizes from the standard sizing guide, ie. Size S will fit sizes 8/10, size M will fit sizes 12/14 and so on.

The sizing within this chart is also based on the larger size within the range, ie. M will be based on size 14.

UK SIZE	S	M	L	XL	
DUAL SIZE	8/10	12/14	16/18	20/22	
To fit bust	32 – 34	36 – 38	40 – 42	44 – 46	inches
	82 – 87	92 – 97	102 – 107	112 – 117	cm
To fit waist	24 – 26	28 – 30	32 – 34	36 – 38	inches
	61 – 66	71 – 76	81 – 86	91 – 96	cm
To fit hips	34 – 36	38 – 40	42 – 44	46 – 48	inches
	87 – 92	97 – 102	107 – 112	117 – 122	cm

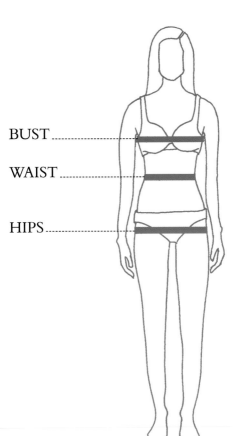

BUST ....

WAIST ....

HIPS ....

MEASURING GUIDE

For maximum comfort and to ensure the correct fit when choosing a size to knit, please follow the tips below when checking your size.

Measure yourself close to your body, over your underwear and don't pull the tape measure too tight!

Bust/chest – measure around the fullest part of the bust/chest and across the shoulder blades.

Waist – measure around the natural waistline, just above the hip bone.

Hips – measure around the fullest part of the bottom.

If you don't wish to measure yourself, note the size of a favourite jumper that you like the fit of. Our sizes are now comparable to the clothing sizes from the major high street retailers, so if your favourite jumper is a size Medium or size 12, then our casual size Medium and standard size 12 should be approximately the same fit.

To be extra sure, measure your favourite jumper and then compare these measurements with the Rowan size diagram given at the end of the individual instructions.

Finally, once you have decided which size is best for you, please ensure that you achieve the tension required for the design you wish to knit.

Remember if your tension is too loose, your garment will be bigger than the pattern size and you may use more yarn. If your tension is too tight, your garment could be smaller than the pattern size and you will have yarn left over.

Furthermore if your tension is incorrect, the handle of your fabric will be too stiff or floppy and will not fit properly. It really does make sense to check your tension before starting every project.

information

TENSION

Obtaining the correct tension is perhaps the single factor which can make the difference between a successful garment and a disastrous one. It controls both the shape and size of an article, so any variation, however slight, can distort the finished garment. Different designers feature in our books and it is **their** tension, given at the **start** of each pattern, which you must match. We recommend that you knit a square in pattern and/or stocking stitch (depending on the pattern instructions) of perhaps 5 - 10 more stitches and 5 - 10 more rows than those given in the tension note. Mark out the central 10cm square with pins. If you have too many stitches to 10cm try again using thicker needles, if you have too few stitches to 10cm try again using finer needles. Once you have achieved the
correct tension your garment will be knitted to the measurements indicated in the size diagram shown at the end of the pattern.

SIZING & SIZE DIAGRAM NOTE

The instructions are given for the smallest size. Where they vary, work the figures in brackets for the larger sizes. **One set of figures refers to all sizes.** Included with most patterns in this magazine is a **'size diagram'**, or sketch of the finished garment and its dimensions. To help you choose the size of garment to knit please refer to the NEW sizing guide on page 102.

CHART NOTE

Many of the patterns in the book are worked from charts. Each square on a chart represents a stitch and each line of squares a row of knitting. Each colour used is given a different letter and these are shown in the **materials** section, or in the **key** alongside the chart of each pattern. When working from the charts, read odd rows (K) from right to left and even rows (P) from left to right, unless otherwise stated. When working lace from a chart it is important to note that all but the largest size may have to alter the first and last few stitches in order not to lose or gain stitches over the row.

WORKING A LACE PATTERN

When working a lace pattern it is important to remember that if you are unable to work both the increase and corresponding decrease and vica versa, the stitches should be worked in stocking stitch.

FINISHING INSTRUCTIONS

After working for hours knitting a garment, it seems a great pity that many garments are spoiled because such little care is taken in the pressing and finishing process. Follow the following tips for a truly professional-looking garment.

PRESSING

Block out each piece of knitting and following the instructions on the ball band press the garment pieces, omitting the ribs. Tip: Take special care to press the edges, as this will make sewing up both easier and neater. If the ball band indicates that the fabric is not to be pressed, then covering the blocked out fabric with a damp white cotton cloth and leaving it to stand will have the desired effect. Darn in all ends neatly along the selvage edge or a colour join, as appropriate.

STITCHING

When stitching the pieces together, remember to match areas of colour and texture very carefully where they meet. Use a seam stitch such as back stitch or mattress stitch for all main knitting seams and join all ribs and neckband with mattress stitch, unless otherwise stated.

CONSTRUCTION

Having completed the pattern instructions, join left shoulder and neckband seams as detailed above. Sew the top of the sleeve to the body of the garment using the method detailed in the pattern, referring to the
appropriate guide:
Straight cast-off sleeves: Place centre of cast-off edge of sleeve to shoulder seam. Sew top of sleeve to body, using markers as guidelines where applicable.
Square set-in sleeves: Place centre of cast-off edge of sleeve to shoulder seam. Set sleeve head into armhole, the straight sides at top of sleeve to form a neat right-angle to cast-off sts at armhole on back and front.
Shallow set-in sleeves: Place centre of cast off edge of sleeve to shoulder seam. Match decreases at beg of armhole shaping to decreases at top of sleeve. Sew sleeve head into armhole, easing in shapings.
Set- in sleeves: Place centre of cast-off edge of sleeve to shoulder seam. Set in sleeve, easing sleeve head into armhole.

Join side and sleeve seams.
Slip stitch pocket edgings and linings into place. Sew on buttons to correspond with buttonholes. Ribbed welts and neckbands and any areas of garter stitch should not be pressed.

= Easy, straight forward knitting

= Suitable for the average knitter

ABBREVIATIONS

K	knit
P	purl
st(s)	stitch(es)
inc	increas(e)(ing)
dec	decreas(e)(ing)
st st	stocking stitch (1 row K , 1 row P)
g st	garter stitch (K every row)
beg	begin(ning)
foll	following
rem	remain(ing)
rev st st	reverse stocking stitch (1 row K , 1 row P)
rep	repeat
alt	alternate
cont	continue
patt	pattern
tog	together
mm	millimetres
cm	centimetres
in(s)	inch(es)
RS	right side
WS	wrong side
sl 1	slip one stitch
psso	pass slipped stitch over
p2sso	pass 2 slipped stitches over
tbl	through back of loop
M1	make one stitch by picking up horizontal loop before next stitch and knitting into back of it
M1P	make one stitch by picking up horizontal loop before next stitch and purling into back of it
yfwd	yarn forward
yrn	yarn round needle
meas	measures
0	no stitches, times or rows
-	no stitches, times or rows for that size
yon	yarn over needle
yfrn	yarn forward round needle
wyib	with yarn at back

AUSTRALIA: Australian Country Spinners, Pty Ltd, Level 7, 409 St. Kilda Road, Melbourne Vic 3004. Tel: 03 9380 3830 Fax: 03 9820 0989 Email: sales@auspinners.com.au

AUSTRIA: Coats Harlander GmbH, Autokaderstrasse 31, A -1210 Wien. Tel: (01) 27716 – 0   Fax: (01) 27716 - 228

BELGIUM: Coats Benelux, Ring Oost 14A, Ninove, 9400, Belgium Tel: 0346 35 37 00 Email: sales.coatsninove@coats.com

CANADA: Westminster Fibers Inc, 165 Ledge St, Nashua, NH03060 Tel: (1 603) 886 5041 / 5043   Fax: (1 603) 886 1056 Email: rowan@westminsterfibers.com

CHINA: Coats Shanghai Ltd, No 9 Building , Baosheng Road, Songjiang Industrial Zone, Shanghai. Tel: (86- 21) 5774 3733   Fax: (86-21) 5774 3768

DENMARK: Coats Danmark A/S, Nannasgade 28, 2200 Kobenhavn N Tel: (45) 35 86 90 50   Fax: (45) 35 82 15 10 Email: info@hpgruppen.dk Web: www.hpgruppen.dk

FINLAND: Coats Opti Oy, Ketjutie 3, 04220 Kerava Tel: (358) 9 274 871   Fax: (358) 9 2748 7330 Email: coatsopti.sales@coats.com

FRANCE: Coats France / Steiner Frères, SAS 100, avenue du Général de Gaulle, 18 500 Mehun-Sur-Yèvre Tel: (33) 02 48 23 12 30   Fax: (33) 02 48 23 12 40

GERMANY: Coats GMbH, Kaiserstrasse 1, D-79341 Kenzingen Tel: (49) 7644 8020   Fax: (49) 7644 802399 Web: www.coatsgmbh.de

HOLLAND: Coats Benelux, Ring Oost 14A, Ninove, 9400, Belgium Tel: 0346 35 37 00 Email: sales.coatsninove@coats.com

HONG KONG: Coats China Holdings Ltd, 19/F Millennium City 2, 378 Kwun Tong Road, Kwun Tong, Kowloon Tel: (852) 2798 6886   Fax: (852) 2305 0311

ICELAND: Storkurinn, Laugavegi 59, 101 Reykjavik Tel: (354) 551 8258 Email: storkurinn@simnet.is

ITALY: Coats Cucirini s.r.l., Via Sarca 223, 20126 Milano Tel: 800 992377   Fax: 0266111701 Email: servizio.clienti@coats.com

KOREA: Coats Korea Co Ltd, 5F Kuckdong B/D, 935-40 Bangbae- Dong, Seocho-Gu, Seoul Tel: (82) 2 521 6262.   Fax: (82) 2 521 5181

LEBANON: y.knot, Saifi Village, Mkhalissiya Street 162, Beirut Tel: (961) 1 992211   Fax: (961) 1 315553 Email: y.knot@cyberia.net.lb

LUXEMBOURG: Coats Benelux, Ring Oost 14A, Ninove, 9400, Belgium Tel: 054 318989 Email: sales.coatsninove@coats.com

MEXICO: Estambres Crochet SA de CV, Aaron Saenz 1891-7, Monterrey, NL 64650 Mexico Tel: +52 (81) 8335-3870

NEW ZEALAND: ACS New Zealand, 1 March Place, Belfast, Christchurch Tel: 64-3-323-6665 Fax: 64-3-323-6660

NORWAY: Coats Knappehuset AS, Pb 100 Ulset, 5873 Bergen Tel: (47) 55 53 93 00   Fax: (47) 55 53 93 93

SINGAPORE: Golden Dragon Store, 101 Upper Cross Street #02-51, People's Park Centre, Singapore 058357 Tel: (65) 6 5358454   Fax: (65) 6 2216278   Email: gdscraft@hotmail.com

SOUTH AFRICA: Arthur Bales PTY, PO Box 44644, Linden 2104 Tel: (27) 11 888 2401   Fax: (27) 11 782 6137

SPAIN: Oyambre, Pau Claris 145, 80009 Barcelona. Tel: (34) 670 011957   Fax: (34) 93 4872672 Email: oyambre@oyambreonline.com

Coats Fabra, Santa Adria 20, 08030 Bercelona Tel: 932908400   Fax: 932908409 Email: atencion.clientes@coats.com

SWEDEN: Coats Expotex AB, Division Craft, Box 297, 401 24 Goteborg Tel: (46) 33 720 79 00   Fax: 46 31 47 16 50

SWITZERLAND: Coats Stroppel AG, Stroppelstr.16 CH -5300 Turgi (AG) Tel: (41) 562981220   Fax: (41) 56 298 12 50

TAIWAN: Cactus Quality Co Ltd, P.O.Box 30 485, Taipei, Taiwan, R.O.C., Office: 7FL-2, No 140, Roosevelt Road, Sec 2, Taipei, Taiwan, R.O.C. Tel: 886-2-23656527 Fax: 886-2-23656503 Email: cqcl@m17.hinet.net

THAILAND: Global Wide Trading, 10 Lad Prao Soi 88, Bangkok 10310 Tel: 00 662 933 9019 Fax: 00 662 933 9110 Email: theneedleworld@yahoo.com

U.S.A.: Westminster Fibers Inc, 165 Ledge St, Nashua, NH03060 Tel: (1 603) 886 5041 / 5043   Fax: (1 603) 886 1056 Email: rowan@westminsterfibers.com

U.K: Rowan, Green Lane Mill, Holmfirth, West Yorkshire, England HD9 2DX Tel: +44 (0) 1484 681881   Fax: +44 (0) 1484 687920 Email: mail@knitrowan.com Web: www.knitrowan.com

For stockists in all other countries please contact Rowan for details

• Photographer: Peter Christian Christensen
• Stylist: Sarah Hatton
• Hair & Make-up: Jeni Dodson
• Model: Marzena Pokrzywinska from Models 1
• Layout: Graham McWilliam & Lisa Richardson

With special thanks to the following handknitters:

Judith Chamberlain, Susan Grimes, Yvonne Rawlinson, Janet Oakey, Arna Ronan, Margaret Goddard,
Glennis Garnet, Jean Fletcher, Anne Newton, Margaret Oswald, Janet Mann, Sandra Taylor

First published in Great Britain in 2008 by Rowan Yarns Ltd, Green Lane Mill, Holmfirth, West Yorkshire, England, HD9 2DX
Internet: www.knitrowan.com
© Copyright Rowan 2008
British Library Cataloguing in Publication Data Rowan Yarns - The Colourscape Chunky Collection
ISBN 978-1-906007-49-2